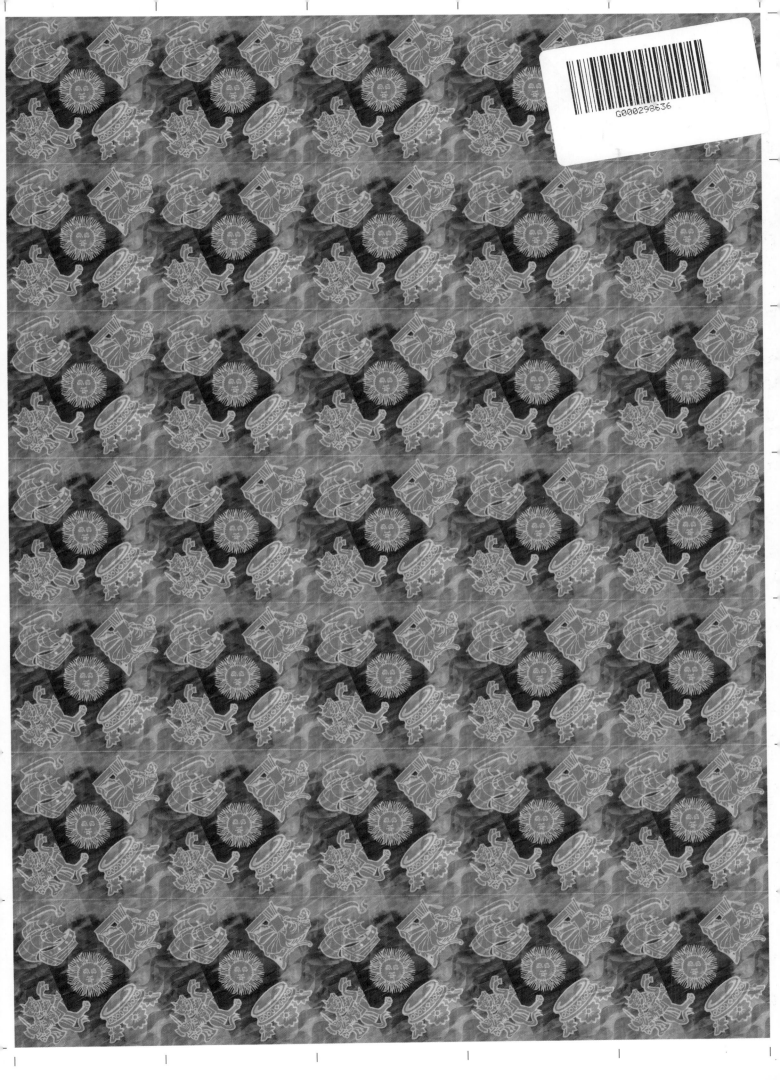

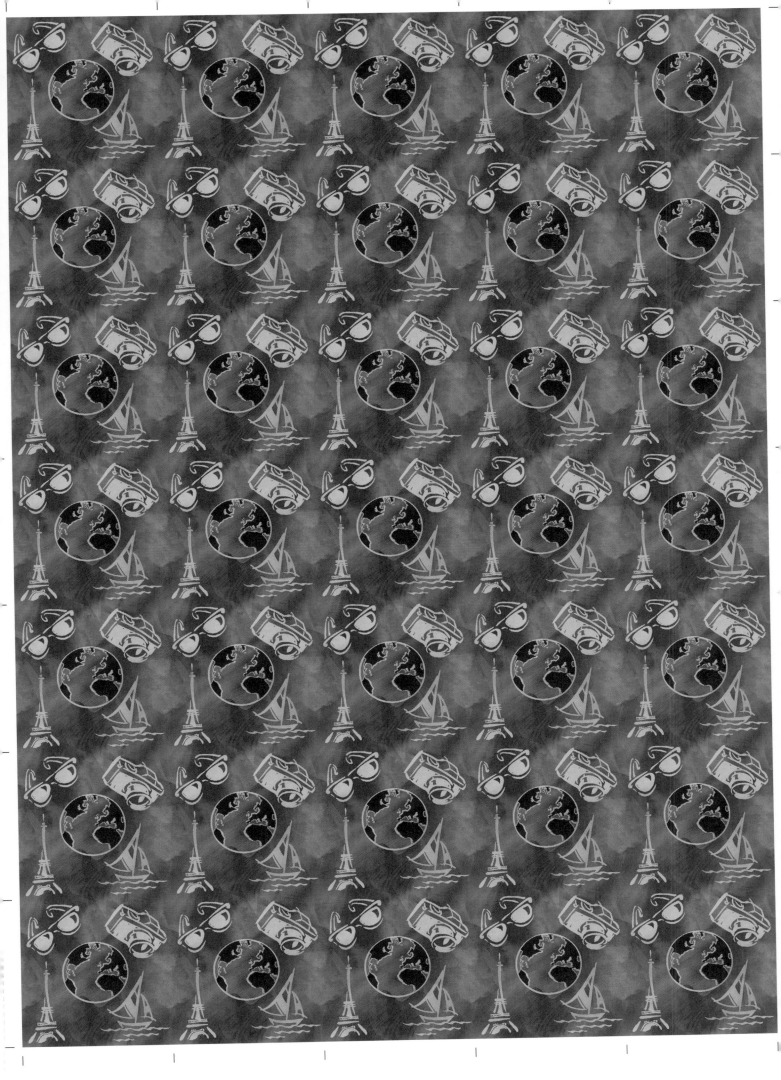

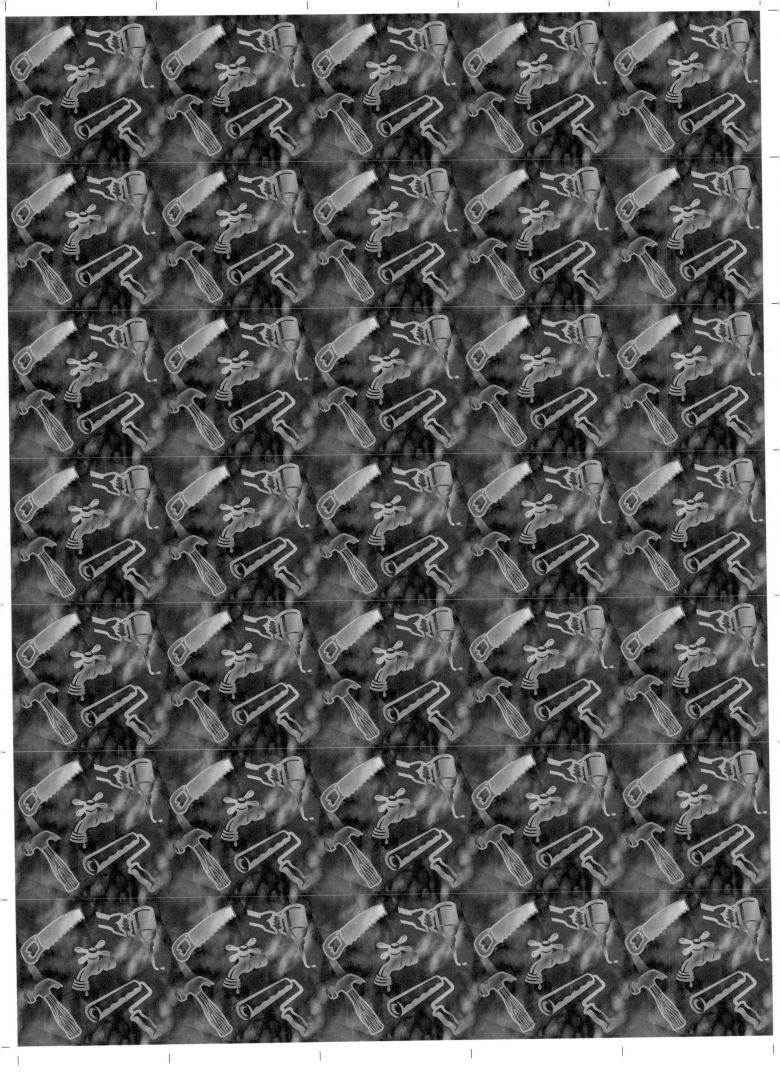

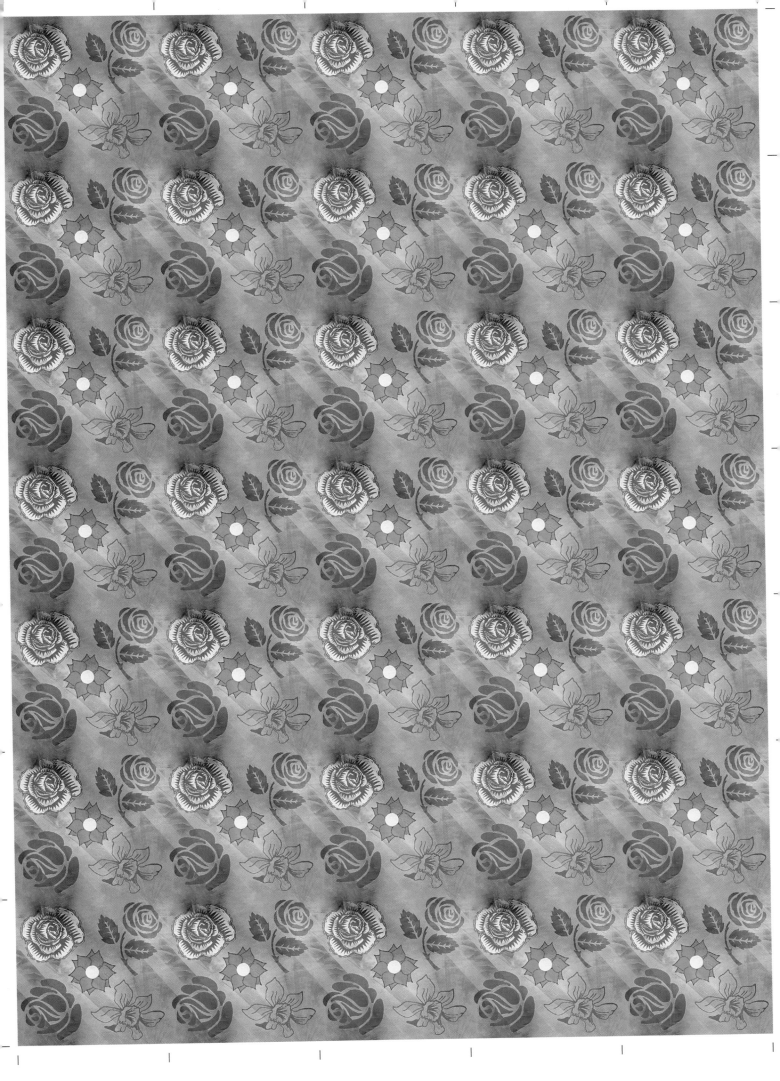

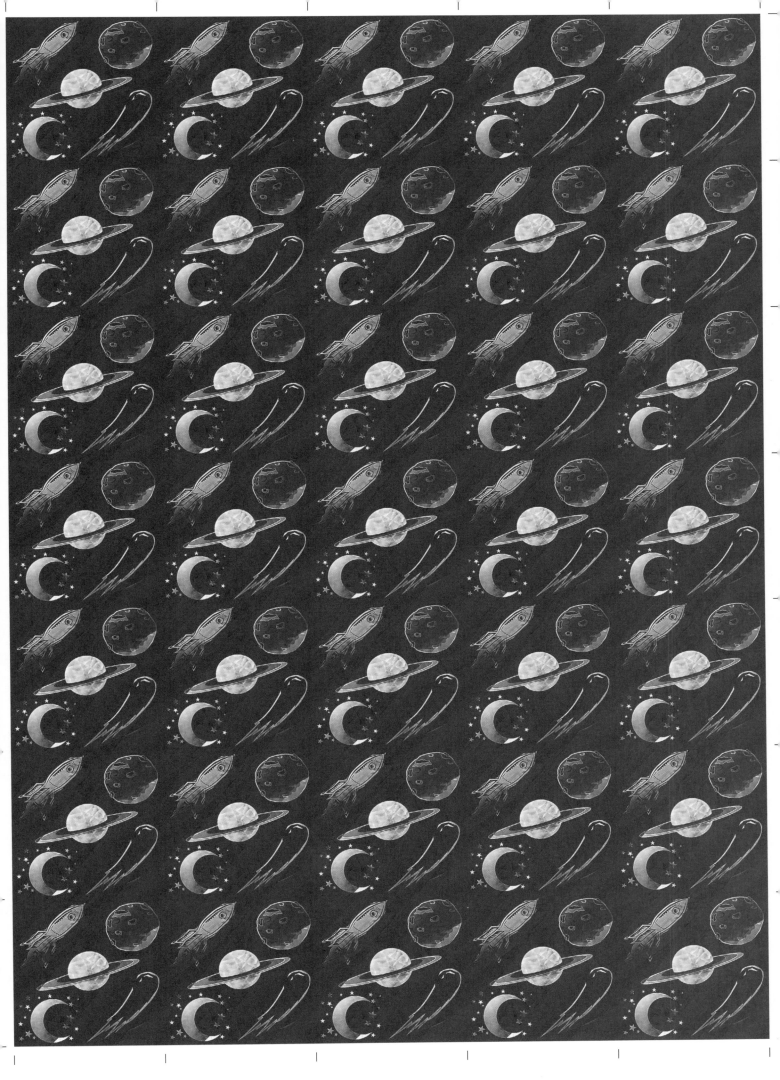

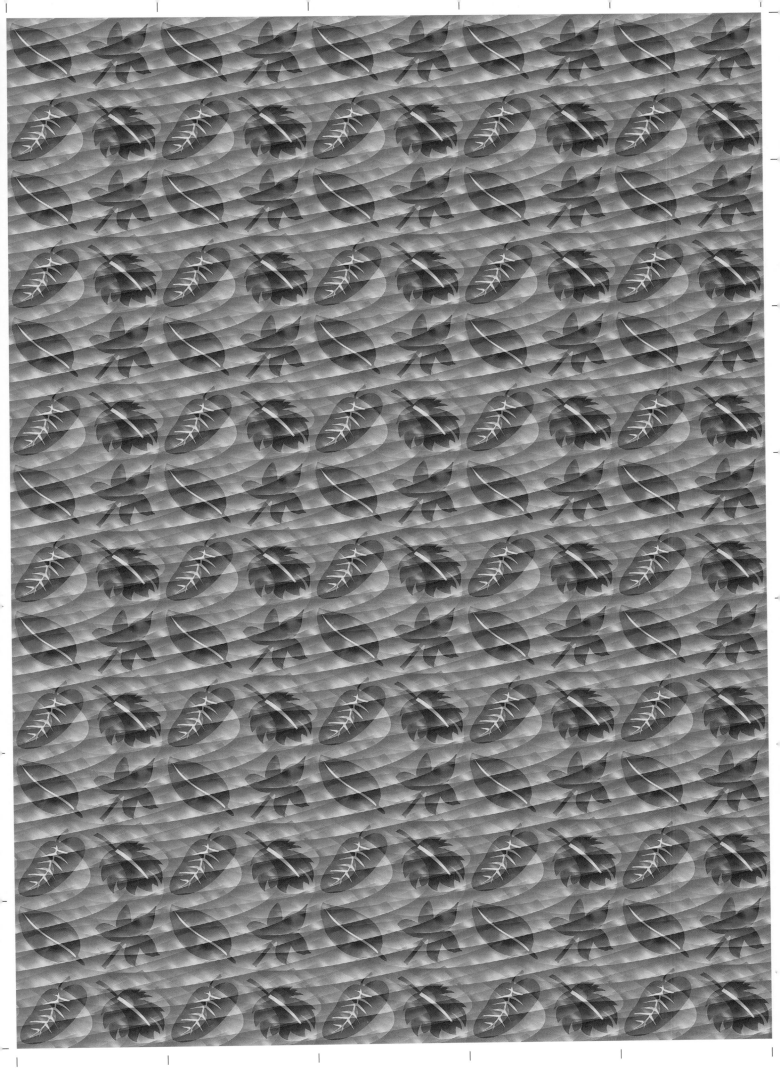

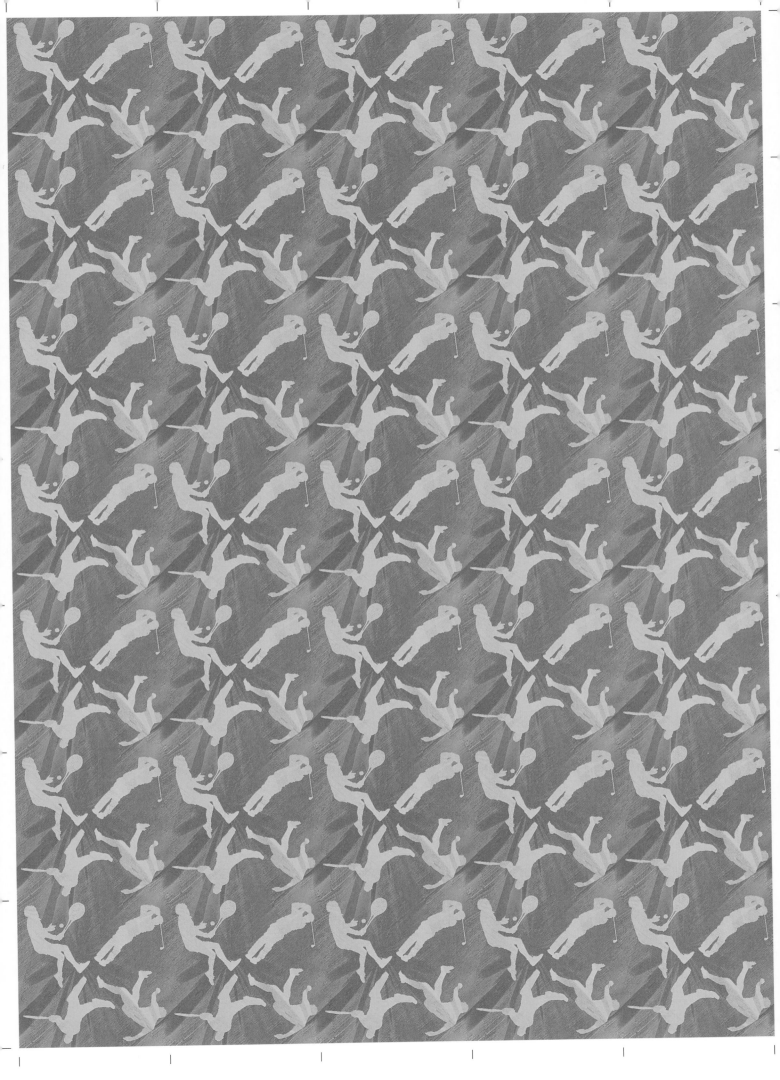

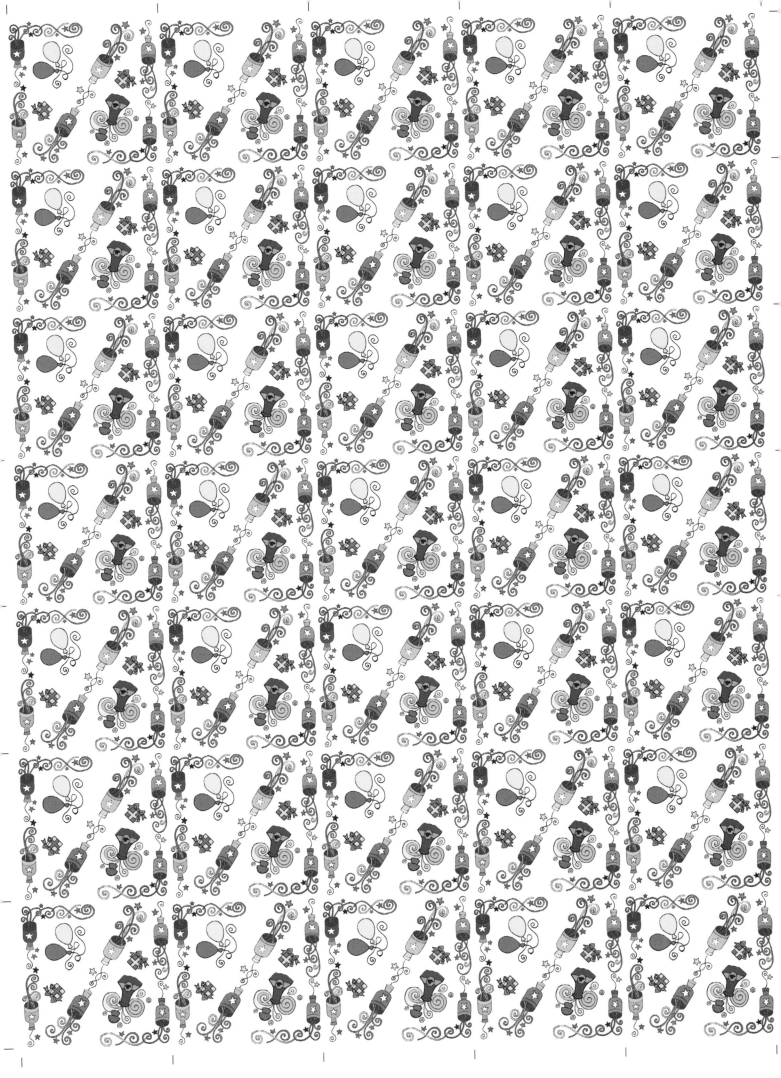

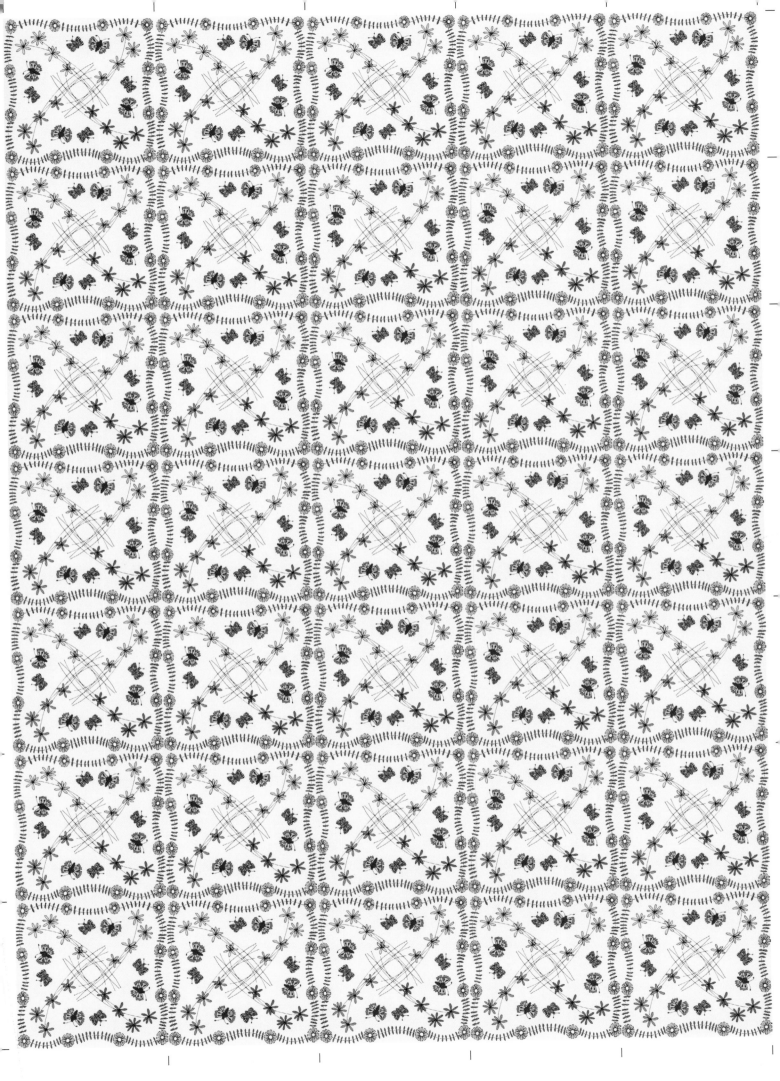

Square Fold
8 Squares

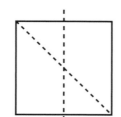

Place each square face down, and fold in half diagonally. Then re-open, and fold in half vertically.

Fold in half again.

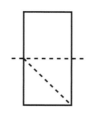

Make sure you use the same corner each time for a kaleidoscopic effect.

Use the original diagonal fold line to help you place the squares accurately. Overlap and glue in position.

Tuck your last square under the first to complete your design.

Rhombus Fold
10 Squares

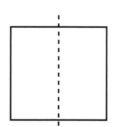

Place each square face down, and fold in half. Then re-open.

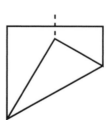

Fold up the bottom corner to touch the middle fold, then re-open.

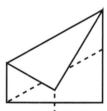

Repeat with the top corner on the opposite side. Re-open.

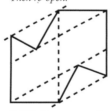

Fold both corners again, to touch the diagonal folds, keeping the new folds parallel.

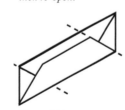

Now refold on your original diagonal folds.

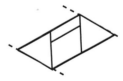

Fold both corners over, to form the finished shape. Overlap and glue all the shapes together as shown.

Kite Fold
10 Squares

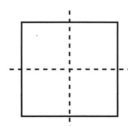

Place each square face down, and fold in half horizontally and then vertically. Re-open.

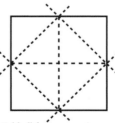

Fold all four corners in diagonally to meet the centre.

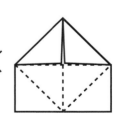

Re-open the bottom two corners.

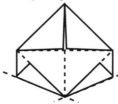

Fold the bottom two corners up to meet the original diagonal fold.

Fold up the bottom corners so that the bottom edges meet at the centre fold.

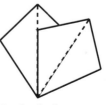

Overlap the shapes as shown, remembering to tuck the last shape under the first, and glue in position.

Pentagon Fold
8 Squares

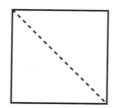

Place each square face down, and fold in half diagonally. Re-open.

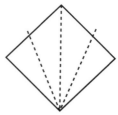

Fold the two opposite corners to meet the centre fold.

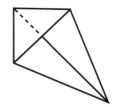

Remember to fold the same way each time to ensure a kaleidoscopic effect.

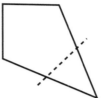

Flip the paper over and fold the longest corner up as shown.

Flatten down to create a pentagonal shape.

Either overlap the shapes or join to make a perfect frame. Glue them in position.

Hexagon Fold
8 Squares

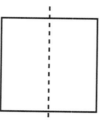

Cut each square in half, keeping matching halves for any one design.

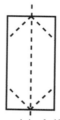

Fold a remaining half square face down in half vertically, and re-open. Fold corners to meet the centre fold.

FINISHED SHAPE 'A'

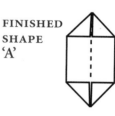

Fold the corners to meet the centre fold.

FINISHED SHAPE 'B'

As an alternative, fold the bottom corners in again so that they meet at the centre.

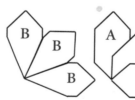

Arrange the finished shapes as shown. Glue them in position.

Star Fold
8 Squares

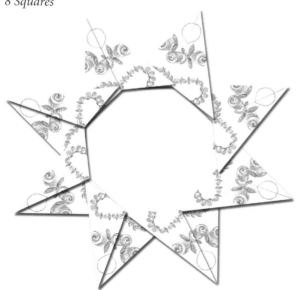

Fold each square in half, with only the white side showing.

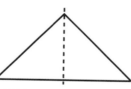

Fold the triangle in half again.

Open up the triangle, and pull the top corner of the outer layer down revealing the printed side. Fold each side of the triangle separately. Press the folds flat on each side, then fold the triangle backwards

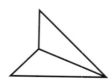

This will result in the basic shape.

Interlock the corners of the shapes to create the final star pattern. Glue in position.

Arrowhead Fold
8 Squares

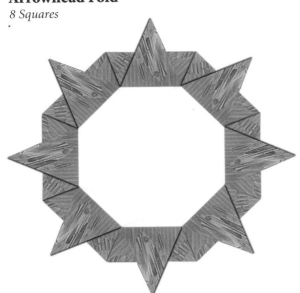

Make sure you use the same corner each time for a kaleidoscopic effect.

Place each square face down, and fold in half diagonally. Fold one corner in to meet the central fold, then the other.

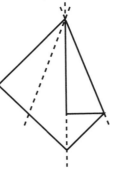

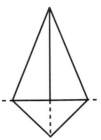

Repeat with the other corner to make a kite shape. Fold up the bottom triangle.

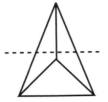

Fold down the top half, so that the corner meets the bottom.

Fold the back of the shape up to meet the top, leaving the point free.

The finished shape. Interlock all the shapes and glue in position.

Leaf Fold
4 Squares

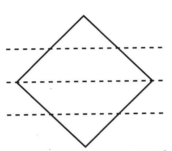

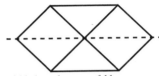

Refold along the centre fold.

Place each square face down, and fold in half diagonally. Re-open. Then fold the top and bottom corners to meet the centre fold.

Make a centre fold and re-open. Fold one side diagonally so that the top meets up with the top of the centre fold.

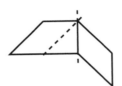

Repeat with the opposite side.

Your shape should now look like this.

Flip over the shape for positioning. Glue all the shapes together.

Butterfly Fold
2 Squares

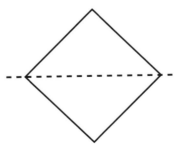

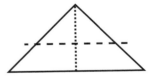

Fold in half again, and re-open. Then fold the top corner down, at just below the halfway point, so that the tip protrudes over the base of the shape.

Place each square face down, and fold in half diagonally.

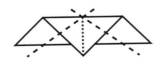

Fold the two halves over at the centre line.

The finished shape. Glue the shapes in position

Tulip Fold
4 Squares

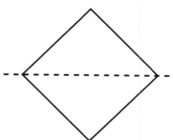

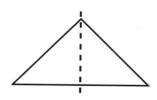

Fold in half again, and re-open, to create a central guide fold

Place each square face down, and fold in half diagonally.

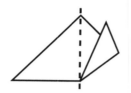

Fold up one corner at about a third away from the tip.

Repeat with the other side to complete the shape. Assemble all the shapes and glue in position

Pyramid Fold
8 Squares

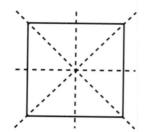

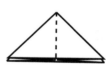

Place each square face down, and fold in half both length ways and diagonally. Then re-open.

On the bottom half of the square, fold the left and right sides in so they meet on the centre fold. Repeat on the other half. Flatten the shape as shown.

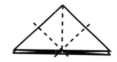

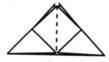

Tuck the two front corners back under themselves.

The completed shape should look like this. Assemble the shapes and glue in position.

Corner Fold
8 Squares

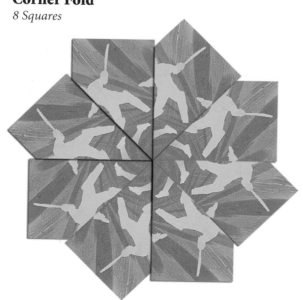

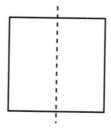

Place each square face down, and fold in half.

Fold diagonally along the angle shown.

Flatten the finished shape as shown. Assemble all the shapes and glue in position.